P9-CRB-080

# MISDEMEANOR PROSECUTION
## YOUR LEGAL RIGHTS

Carla Mooney

**ROSEN**
PUBLISHING

New York

Published in 2015 by The Rosen Publishing Group, Inc.
29 East 21st Street, New York, NY 10010

**Expert Reviewer:** Lindsay A. Lewis, Esq.

**Library of Congress Cataloging-in-Publication Data**

Mooney, Carla, 1970– author.
Misdemeanor prosecution: your legal rights/Carla Mooney.
    p. cm.—(Know your rights)
Includes bibliographical references and index.
ISBN 978-1-4777-8028-2 (library bound) —
ISBN 978-1-4777-8029-9 (pbk.) — ISBN 978-1-4777-8030-5 (6-pack)
1. Criminal law—United States—Juvenile literature. 2. Crime—United
States—Juvenile literature. I. Title.
KF9219.85.M66 2014
345.73'02—dc23

2014010579

*Manufactured in the United States of America*

# CONTENTS

Introduction . . . . . . . . . . . . . . . . . . . . . . . . . . . 4

Chapter 1
**What Are Misdemeanors and Minor Offenses?** . . . . . . . . . . . . . . . . . . . 7

Chapter 2
**What Happens When I Receive a Citation?** . . . . . . . . . . . . 15

Chapter 3
**Preparing for Court** . . . . . . . . . . . 24

Chapter 4
**What to Expect at Court** . . . . . 33

Chapter 5
**Avoiding Trouble in the Future** . . . . . . . . . . . . . . . . . . . . . 43

Glossary . . . . . . . . . . . . . . . . . . . . . . . . . . . . . . 55

For More Information . . . . . . . . . . . . . . . . . . . . 57

For Further Reading . . . . . . . . . . . . . . . . . . . . . 59

Bibliography . . . . . . . . . . . . . . . . . . . . . . . . . . . 60

Index . . . . . . . . . . . . . . . . . . . . . . . . . . . . . . . . . 61

# INTRODUCTION

Sometimes a simple prank lands you in hot water with the law. Like many teens, Zayd, Faysal, and Omar Khatib from Virginia enjoyed practical jokes. The two brothers and their cousin decided to start filming their pranks. They started their own YouTube channel and posted about twenty videos for others to watch. Some videos showed the teens lying down in odd poses on a moving elevator. In another video, the teens pretended to splash unknowing bystanders with an empty bucket.

In 2013, the teens designed a new prank to film. Over the course of six days, the three of them shot video of themselves smashing gallon containers of milk and juice in local grocery stores. They pretended to trip and fall. Gallons of milk crashed dramatically to the floor. The teens flailed in the spilled milk, while bystanders rushed to their aid and did not know that the prank was being filmed.

The teens posted the gallon smashing video on YouTube in February 2013. The video gathered three million views in only three days. It became one of their most popular pranks. The teens said the prank was harmless fun. No one was hurt.

Some people who watched the video thought that it was funny. Yet others said that the prank crossed the line. Dana Cole is an attorney and legal analyst for ABC News. She says the prank could be a criminal act. Cole said it

*A girl clowns around and poses for a picture. When driving, seemingly harmless fun can quickly get out of hand and lead to a traffic violation or car accident.*

seemed malicious and not funny because someone had to clean it up. Because of that, it could be viewed as a crime.

Outraged viewers e-mailed Virginia police about the video. Although the teens eventually removed the video from YouTube, it was too late. Other people had reposted the clips on other Internet sites. The police studied the online video. They agreed that the teens had broken the law. In 2013, the Fairfax County, Virginia, police charged all three youths with seven counts of disorderly conduct and destruction of property.

Many youths across the country find themselves in similar trouble with the law. They are caught speeding or driving without a license. A store clerk catches them shoplifting. A little fun gets out of hand and results in property damage. Even activities that many people don't expect to cause trouble—such as cutting through the park after sundown, drinking an alcoholic beverage on the sidewalk or at the beach, or urinating in public—can lead to a run-in with the law.

If you suddenly find yourself charged with a misdemeanor or a minor offense (including traffic infractions or violations), it can be a scary time. What does a misdemeanor mean? What can you expect in court? And how will being charged with a misdemeanor affect your future?

When faced with uncertainty, knowledge is power. Even though it may seem overwhelming, the legal system can be navigated if you have the right information. Knowing what to expect can help you reach the best possible outcome

# CHAPTER 1

# WHAT ARE MISDEMEANORS AND MINOR OFFENSES?

In August 2012, the family of sixteen-year-old Bobby Lopez Jr. received a series of troubling texts. The texts stated that the teenager from Syracuse, New York, had been kidnapped and was in trouble. Lopez's family immediately contacted the police to report the alleged kidnapping. The Syracuse police began an intense search for the teen. About eight hours later, they found Lopez safe at a relative's house.

The police investigation discovered that Lopez himself sent the alarming texts to his family. The police said that Lopez's prank put city residents at risk. Because the police were spending their time and efforts searching for him, other areas that truly needed police services may not have received them. As a result, the police charged Lopez with a misdemeanor crime for faking his own abduction. He was ordered to appear in court at a later time.

Lopez was charged with falsely reporting an incident, a misdemeanor charge. So what does that mean? State legislatures classify offenses according to how serious they are. They also consider the offenses' impact on victims and

*The police search for evidence near a crime scene in a Chicago, Illinois, neighborhood. The evidence they find will help determine the severity of the offense and the corresponding charges.*

society. Offenses generally fall into three main categories: violations, misdemeanors, and felonies.

# VIOLATIONS

The least serious type of offense is a violation. Violations are not considered crimes. The punishment for a violation is generally a fine, community service, or enrollment in a court-sponsored course. Most traffic infractions, such as failing to stop at a stop sign or red light, fall into this category.

Because a violation is not considered a crime, it does not become a part of a person's criminal record. In most states, you also do not have the right to a jury trial, as violations do not generally result in a jail sentence. If you are charged with a violation, the government does not have to appoint a lawyer for you. If you choose, you can hire your own lawyer to defend you.

# MISDEMEANORS

A misdemeanor is more serious than a violation. Examples of misdemeanor crimes include a first-time DUI (driving under the influence of alcohol or drugs), simple assault, public drunkenness, or shoplifting. Some states divide misdemeanor crimes into classes or degrees. These classifications affect the type of punishment.

People convicted of a misdemeanor crime can be punished by up to one year in jail. Other punishments for misdemeanor crimes include payment of fines, probation, community service, and restitution. People charged with a misdemeanor crime have the right to a jury trial. If they can't afford to hire a lawyer to defend them, the government will appoint a lawyer to their case.

# FELONIES

A felony is the most serious type of crime. It usually involves serious physical harm or the threat of harm to victims. Examples of felonies include assault with a deadly weapon or the sale of illegal drugs. Some felonies are theft and fraud schemes. Sometimes misdemeanor

Some police departments will issue a citation for littering, trespassing, disorderly conduct, or criminal mischief to teens caught toilet-papering a tree or house, especially if the homeowner's property is damaged.

crimes can be classified as a felony if the defendant is a second-time offender.

Felonies are punishable by fines and possibly imprisonment of more than a year. Some felonies can be punished by life in prison without parole. In certain cases, there is the possibility of being sentenced to probation. In that case, the defendant is monitored for a period of time set by the court, and he or she must adhere to certain terms, including that he or she must not commit any further crimes. In some states, a felony such as a gruesome murder can be punished by the death penalty. Like misdemeanors, states can classify felonies by class or degree. People charged with felonies have the right to a jury trial.

# CLASSES OF MISDEMEANORS

Most states classify misdemeanors into subcategories. These categories are determined by the seriousness of the crime. Generally, misdemeanors are classified by numbers or letters. For example, the first category may be called Class 1 or Class A.

Class 1 or Class A misdemeanors are usually the most serious offenses. They carry greater punishment. If convicted of a Class 1 misdemeanor, a defendant may face a fine of up to $5,000 and a jail sentence of up to twelve months. Class 4 or Class D misdemeanors are usually the least serious. Punishment may include a maximum fine of $500 and a jail sentence of up to thirty days. Many states, however, do not require jail time for Class 4 and even Class 3 misdemeanors.

Sometimes misdemeanor offenses may not be classified at all. They are called unclassified misdemeanors.

The court usually deals with these offenses on a case-by-case basis. The judge may use his or her discretion to assign a punishment.

Some states have minor misdemeanors. Examples of minor misdemeanors are speeding violations and other minor citations. These offenses are not usually punished with jail time and only incur a small fine.

When a person is charged with a misdemeanor, he or she has the right to a jury trial. Misdemeanors are usually tried in the lowest local court. This can be a municipal, police, or juvenile court.

## COMMON MISDEMEANOR CRIMES

Misdemeanor offenses can be a variety of crimes. Some of the most common misdemeanor crimes include petty theft, public intoxication, simple assault, and trespassing.

Petty theft occurs when a defendant takes someone's property against his or her will. He or she may take a car, a piece of jewelry, a computer, or money. In most states, petty theft is defined as a theft under $500. If a defendant steals property that is worth more than $500, the crime becomes grand theft and can be classified as a felony.

When people drink alcohol or use drugs, they can become impaired and cause a disturbance in a private or public place. The punishment for public intoxication varies from state to state. In some states, such as California and Kansas, an impaired person can be arrested for public intoxication, which is considered a misdemeanor. In states such as Nevada and Montana, there is no public intoxication law.

## WHO IS A MINOR?

In 1971, the Twenty-sixth Amendment to the U.S. Constitution set the age of majority in the United States to eighteen. The age of majority is the age at which a person has full legal responsibility for himself or herself. In a few states, the age of majority is higher, such as in Alabama (nineteen) and Mississippi (twenty-one). In most states, a minor or juvenile is someone who is under the age of eighteen. As a minor, a person is restricted in some actions, including voting in elections, entering a binding contract, or joining the military without parental consent.

Minors who get in trouble with the law have a separate court system. Juvenile courts have many different names depending on the state and jurisdiction. In Los Angeles, there is a juvenile delinquency court, a dependency court, and an informal juvenile and traffic court. Depending on the state, most juvenile courts will hear cases for minors up to the age of seventeen. Beyond that age, the court may decide that a defendant can be tried in adult court.

Simple assault is another common misdemeanor charge. Simple assault is an assault without the intent of injury. Invading another person's personal space can be an example of simple assault. When the assault involves a police officer, elected officials, or social workers, it becomes a more serious felony charge.

When a person enters, walks on, or lives in private property without permission, he or she can be charged with trespassing. Trespassing laws vary from state to state and jurisdiction to jurisdiction. Most states treat trespassing as a misdemeanor crime.

Other examples of common misdemeanors include disturbing the police, various traffic violations, driving

A school maintenance department worker uses a power washer to remove graffiti on the school building. A senior prank turned into vandalism when the students used paint instead of chalk.

without a license, carrying fake identification, vandalism, and shoplifting.

## WHAT'S NEXT?

After being arrested for a misdemeanor, a person may only have to pay a fine. Even so, having a misdemeanor conviction on your permanent record can affect your future. That's why it is important to understand the court process and what you can expect.

CHAPTER 2

# WHAT HAPPENS WHEN I RECEIVE A CITATION?

In 2013, a police officer was patrolling in Saline, Michigan. He noticed a teen acting suspiciously behind a town building at around 10:40 PM. The teen was standing next to a building with fresh graffiti. The officer approached the youth and asked what he was holding behind his back. The teen revealed a can of black spray paint and confessed to spraying graffiti on the building, as well as on another town building earlier that same night. The officer arrested the teen. The teen eventually confessed to seven additional graffiti cases. He was charged with multiple counts of malicious destruction of property, a misdemeanor crime in Michigan. The teen faced punishment of up to ninety-three days in jail and a $500 fine if found guilty of the charges.

## LAW ENFORCEMENT

Many people will find themselves stopped by law enforcement. They may have broken the law unintentionally by driving distractedly or disturbing the peace. Other times, they may have done something they knew was wrong, like shoplifting or driving without a license. In any of these situations, a person may find himself or herself face-to-face with law enforcement. For many people,

A young man paints graffiti on the side of a building. If caught by police, he could be charged with a misdemeanor crime in many jurisdictions across the United States.

being stopped by the police is a scary experience. Knowing who they are and what to expect can help make the situation less scary.

Law enforcement officers or police officers can work for several different agencies. Some are part of a local community's police force. Others work for the county sheriff's department or the state highway patrol. In addition, some law enforcement officers work as park rangers, school police, housing police, parking officers, metro police, beach patrol, ski patrol, and as employees of other agencies. Any of these officers can stop a person and issue a citation or fine for a violation of local or state law.

## SIGNALED TO STOP

You're driving down the road when suddenly you see flashing red lights in your rearview mirror. A loud siren blares behind you. A police car follows you. What should you do?

Immediately, you should slow down. Look for a safe place to pull off the road. Use your blinker to signal to the officer that you plan to pull over. Then stop on the side of the road as soon as it is safe.

Once you've stopped, remain seated. You should wait in your car for the officer to approach you. If you try to get out of the car, the officer may see it as a threat. It can take a few minutes before the officer approaches. Often a police officer will enter a car's license plate into a computer to check if it has been reported stolen or if there are any outstanding citations on it. While waiting for the officer, roll down your window. You should also keep both hands on the steering wheel where the officer can see them. Do not reach to grab something out of your purse or glove compartment until the officer asks you to do so. If you move suddenly, the officer may suspect that you are reaching for a weapon.

When the officer approaches, stay calm. Getting upset or arguing will not help the situation. It is important to remain respectful and polite, even if you believe that you have done nothing wrong. In the same way, if you are approached by a police officer on the street, follow a similar plan. Stop immediately and be respectful. Listen carefully to the officer's instructions. Keep your hands in

*A young woman waits in her car after being pulled over by the police. The police officer will check her license plate number to see if the car is stolen or has any outstanding citations.*

view of the officer. If you touch or threaten a police officer, you can land in even more trouble. The officer may arrest you and charge you with additional crimes.

## RECEIVING A CITATION

Sometimes the police officer will issue a citation or ticket, also known in some states as a summons. Many driving violations receive citations. A citation or summons is a notice to appear in court on a later date. The officer will ask you to sign your citation. Signing the citation does not mean that you are guilty. Signing simply means that you have received it. A citation or summons is, in fact, an indication that you have not been arrested. If you refuse to sign the citation, the officer will be forced to arrest you and take you to a police station.

In New York City, there is something similar to a citation or summons that is known as a desk appearance ticket (DAT). A DAT is given to individuals who are indeed arrested, but released before being taken to central booking (where fingerprints, a mug shot, and processing occur). Just as it is with a citation, people who have received a DAT must appear in court at a later date.

After you sign a citation, the officer will give you a copy. Different law enforcement agencies use different tickets, but most have the same basic parts. The citation will record several pieces of information. It will list the date, time, and place the alleged offense occurred. It should also have the code section or statute that was violated. If a car was involved, the citation will have details about the car, such as the vehicle identification number (VIN), make and model, and registration. The citation will also list information about you, including your name, address, gender, height, weight, age, birth date, and other descriptions. The citation will have the name of the officer, his or her police station, and badge number. The officer will sign and date the citation.

After you receive a citation, it is important to read the text on the citation. A citation or summons will instruct the recipient when and where to appear if he or she wishes to contest it. Sometimes it is not necessary to appear in person. A person can often plead guilty by mail. Sometimes,

## PROBABLE CAUSE

When a police officer stops you, he or she must have probable cause. This means that the officer must have a specific reason for stopping you. Maybe the officer saw you ignore a stop sign or found you at an underage drinking party. Probable cause can also include violations with your car, like an expired registration sticker or a broken headlight.

Just because an officer has probable cause to stop you doesn't necessarily mean that he or she has probable cause to search your body, belongings, or vehicle. There are certain limitations on what probable cause allows an officer to do. An officer cannot, for example, search your trunk or glove compartment without a warrant stating so.

regardless of whether or not you plan to contest the ticket, you must appear in court. Failure to appear will result in a bench warrant for your arrest. Always read a citation or summons very carefully for instructions.

# UNDERSTANDING YOUR CITATION

Citations are frequently used for violations or misdemeanor crimes. The citation states what violation you are being accused of committing. When you receive a citation, you should always make sure that you understand exactly what law you're accused of having violated. The citation will have a code section written on it. You can look up the code section at your local library, county law library, or on the Internet. This information will help you understand the charges against you. Using the code section, you can also make sure that the officer did not make any errors on the citation.

While most citations are accurate, mistakes do occur. Most of the time, written mistakes on a citation do not cause a judge to dismiss the charges. Most errors are considered minor. Many times if there is a minor error, the officer can send you an amendment or correction in the mail. For example, writing the wrong time on a citation for missing a stop sign is a minor error. Other times, an error on a citation is significant. If the code section on the citation does not match the narrative written by the officer, or the ticket does not allege all of the elements of the crime charged, a judge may decide to dismiss the charges. The type of error and how important it is to the violation will determine if the mistake is significant.

# DETENTION AND ARREST

In some situations, a police officer may detain you for questioning after you've been pulled over. For some misdemeanor crimes, the officer will arrest you. If you are arrested, the officer is required to advise you of your Miranda rights before questioning you. Miranda rights are based on a 1966 Supreme Court ruling in *Miranda v. Arizona*. The Court ruled that citizens had certain constitutional rights when arrested and questioned by police. Your Miranda rights include the right to remain silent, the right to speak with a lawyer, and the right to have a lawyer with you during police questioning.

While many people are familiar with these rights from television shows and movies, these rights are not always issued as they are in the movies. Sometimes Miranda warnings are not given until you are already at a police station or talking with an officer. Therefore, if you are not sure whether you are under arrest, it is important to ask. If you are under arrest, or if you are not sure if you are under arrest, the best

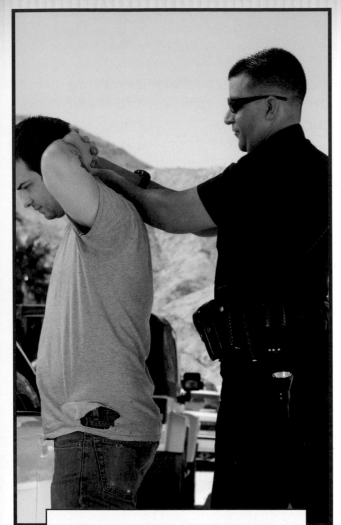

*A police officer arrests a young man before taking him to the police station for detention and questioning. Before questioning can begin, the officer must read the detainee his Miranda rights.*

practice is to state that you have the right to remain silent and that you will not say anything further until you have been given a lawyer and that lawyer is present.

# REPORTS AND STATEMENTS

There are several types of reports that may be written and filed about a misdemeanor or minor crime. In some cases, the officer involved will prepare a police report. A police report will contain a narrative about the incident. It includes observations from the officer. It may also include the names, addresses, and statements from witnesses at the scene. You have the right to see a copy of the police report. The police might also produce a copy of a statement from you. Whether made intentionally or as off-hand comments at the time of arrest, a copy of any statement you make must be provided to you and your attorney.

The police report about your case may include witness statements or a traffic collision report. If there are witnesses at the scene, the police will take a witness statement. A witness statement describes what the witness saw and heard in detail. A traffic collision report records information about the accident. It details the weather conditions, lighting, road conditions, and any other factors that may have played a role in the accident. It also states the person most at fault. You should try to get a copy of each report related to your case before you go to court.

# CHAPTER 3

# PREPARING FOR COURT

After you've been charged with a misdemeanor or minor crime, you will be given a date and time to appear in court. You can use the time before your court date to prepare for your case. Having as much information as possible before you walk into court can help your case.

## COURT DATE AND TIME

You should make every effort to appear in court at your scheduled time. Sometimes there are legitimate reasons why you cannot be there. Your parents might be out of town for work. Your school could be administering state tests. Or perhaps you have a medical problem that prevents you from going to court.

If you have a legitimate conflict, some jurisdictions allow a continuance. A continuance is a postponement of your original court date. Depending on the jurisdiction, you can request a continuance by phone, mail, or in person. Always keep a record of your communication with the court. Write down the names of the people you talk to and the dates and times you called. If you send a letter, consider asking for a delivery confirmation or signature to prove that you sent it. If you are granted a continuance, you will get a new court date.

If your request is not granted, you are responsible to appear in court on your originally scheduled date.

As an alternative, if you have counsel, he or she may be able to appear on your behalf in some instances. Generally, this will require you to sign a waiver of appearance authorizing your lawyer to act on your behalf, and possibly even to resolve the case for you. If you know you cannot make a court date and you have counsel, you should contact them as soon as possible to discuss your options. As a general rule, however, it is always better to appear in court yourself (even when your lawyer tells you that he or she can do the appearance without you).

Sometimes a last-minute problem may cause you to miss your court date. If you miss a court date for any reason, you should immediately contact the court and return to court promptly to avoid more serious consequences. When you return to court, make sure that you have proof of why you missed your original court date. If an unexpected medical problem landed you in the hospital, have the doctor or hospital write a letter explaining what happened. If your employer sent you on a last-minute business trip, bring a letter from the employer, airline tickets, and any other travel documents.

Failure to appear in court on the scheduled date and time can lead to serious consequences. In many cases, the judge can issue a bench warrant for your arrest. Other times, the court can charge you with a failure-to-appear offense. The failure-to-appear offense will be added to your existing charges. In addition, if you are charged with a driving offense, the court can tell the Department of Motor Vehicles (DMV) to suspend your driving privileges.

# PREPARING DOCUMENTS FOR COURT

Before your court date, you should spend time preparing. Are there any documents that you want to present to the court or the prosecutor? Some documents such as licenses, permits, or training certificates are required for your hearing. Receipts and letters from an authorized auto repair shop prove that you have fixed car registration or equipment problems. Proof of insurance can also be required for driving violations. Being prepared in court can mean the difference between a larger fine and a smaller one.

In the event that you are found guilty and are facing sentencing (either after a trial or as part of a plea deal), your attorney may recommend other documents that show evidence of your good behavior and character. The court may consider these documents when deciding the severity of your punishment. School records can show that you work hard for good grades and that you attend school regularly. You can also bring character references, including letters from teachers, employers, coaches, clergy, or other respected adults in your life. In the letter, your reference may talk about your positive qualities and give evidence of your good citizenship.

Documents that show you are a productive member of society can also be helpful in court. College acceptances and military papers show that you are responsible and have goals for the future. Proof of employment shows responsibility and that you are working to be a productive member of society.

A good first step to preparing documents for court is to ask your lawyer which, if any, of these documents or

*When charged with a misdemeanor or certain minor offenses, you will be summoned to court. In the courtroom, you will have the opportunity to present your version of the events surrounding the misdemeanor or minor offense.*

character references might help improve the outcome of your case. Oftentimes these documents can be presented to the prosecuting attorney ahead of court appearances. Offering helpful evidence or demonstrating a willingness to seek counseling (such as anger or drug or alcohol abuse counseling) can be used as leverage to negotiate a better outcome with the prosecutor. A more favorable sentence or even a complete dismissal of charges may arise if you present the right evidence. Judges tend to defer to a prosecutor's offer, so ask your counsel the best way to negotiate with the prosecution.

## TRIAL BY DECLARATION

Some courts allow you to request a trial by declaration. In a trial by declaration, you do not have to appear in court for a trial. You waive your right to appear in court, call witnesses, and testify in person. Instead, you complete a written statement on a special form. Your statement explains the facts in your case. It also explains why the court should rule in your favor. Sometimes the written statement can be mailed. Other times, you deliver it in person. In addition, you can attach any evidence to your statement that you think would help the judge decide the case in your favor.

Other documents show the court that you are sorry for the incident and have changed your ways. For example, if you were arrested for a drug-related charge, you may bring clean drug test results from an approved doctor or lab to court. This evidence shows the court that you are not doing drugs at the time of the hearing.

A letter from a therapist or rehabilitation facility can also tell the court that you are trying to make positive changes in your life. A letter to the judge can show the court that you are sorry for what you have done and have taken the time to think about your actions. If you decide to write an apology letter to the victim, if any, you should give the court a copy to show your remorse and that you have attempted to make amends.

# WHO TO BRING TO COURT

If you are a minor, a parent or legal guardian will come with you to court. A legal guardian is an adult given written permission by your parents to be your guardian. A legal guardian can also be appointed by the court. You cannot bring an older sibling, boyfriend or girlfriend, aunt, uncle, or older friend to court. The person must be authorized as a legal guardian.

In one case, Sam B. did not want to tell his parents about a trespassing citation. He brought his older brother to his court hearing. He lied to the court and claimed that his parents were out of town and could not be contacted.

*A young woman talks to her lawyer about her case. A lawyer is the person assigned or hired to help you prepare and present your case in court.*

Sam's excuse was recorded in his court file. The court told him to return at a later date with his parents or a proper authorization from his parents to appoint a legal guardian. When Sam returned to court with his parents the next day, his false statements hurt his believability in court.

Sometimes parents cannot attend a hearing because of a valid reason. They may be sick or in the hospital. They may be out of town or unable to leave their jobs. In these circumstances, the parents can appoint a temporary guardian for court. They will prepare a

## PRE-HEARING CONTRACT

In some cases, a minor may be able to avoid going to court by signing a pre-hearing contract. In these cases, the district attorney's office can review the case before it goes to court. He or she may recommend that the minor defendant and the district attorney's office make a contract instead of having a court hearing. In the contract, the minor admits that he or she acted improperly. The minor accepts responsibility for his or her actions. The minor and his or her parents agree to the terms of the contract. The contract may require the minor to have good grades and school attendance. He or she may have to participate in counseling or perform community service. The minor may also have to complete drug and alcohol treatment. If the minor fails to meet the conditions of the agreement, the court can file a petition against him or her. The district attorney will monitor the agreement for a period of time, usually one year.

written authorization that you will bring to court. They may also include a letter from their employer or doctor explaining why they cannot be in court.

If you do not get along or live with your parents, they may be still legally responsible for you. If they refuse to come to court, the court will assign a social worker or another adult to take their place. In some cases, close relatives, social workers, or a placement worker who is familiar with your history should come to court with you.

In some cases, you do not have to appear with an adult. If you turn

*A young man stands before a judge in the courtroom. The judge may ask him several questions about the charges against him and the circumstances surrounding the crime.*

eighteen between your citation and your court date, some courts will allow you to appear without a parent or guardian. If you are an emancipated minor, you may come to court without a parent. An emancipated minor has been released from parental authority by a court. In this case, you will be required to provide proof of emancipation.

# DO YOU NEED AN ATTORNEY?

The decision to hire an attorney is different for every person, every case. You should discuss this with your parents, guardian, or other trusted adult. Whether you need an attorney depends on the offense and how serious it is. Many misdemeanors and infractions do not need to involve an attorney. If you are charged with a more serious misdemeanor and face possible jail time, you may want to consult an attorney. One scenario in which you may also want to consult an attorney is if you are not a citizen. This is because your case may have consequences on your ability to remain a resident. In fact, even if you hire or have a court-appointed criminal attorney, an immigration lawyer may also be necessary to help you avoid undesirable consequences regarding your immigration status that could result from a conviction or violation. The crime or offense could lead to deportation or prevent you from becoming a citizen in the future.

Another scenario in which it may be best to consult an attorney is if you are on or will seek financial aid or public benefits, or if you plan to work in certain careers. Anybody who wants to be in the military, become a police officer, work in a government agency, be a doctor or lawyer, attend graduate school, or work in finance may have difficulties depending on the outcome of his or her case. A lawyer can inform you of the consequences and how a case (even a dismissal) will appear on your record. You can ask your local bar association or the American Bar Association for a referral to a local attorney who works with juvenile or similar cases.

# CHAPTER 4

# WHAT TO EXPECT AT COURT

Your day in court has arrived. You're nervous and wondering what will happen. Knowing what to expect at court can help you achieve the most positive outcome.

## ARRIVING TO COURT

The first step toward making a good impression is dressing appropriately for your court appearance. You should wear clothing that is neat, clean, and respectful for your court appearance. Clothing that has alcohol or drug references is inappropriate. Revealing clothing, gang attire, or sagging pants should not be worn. You should also leave hats and hoods at home, unless you wear a head covering for religious reasons. In addition, sunglasses, cameras, gum, and cell phones are often not allowed in the courtroom. If you arrive at court in improper dress, you may not be allowed to appear before the judge.

It is also important to arrive at court on time. The citation will have a designated time for your court appearance. You can find directions to the courthouse online—either on the court's website or through an Internet search. If you are driving, research where you are going to park. Allow extra

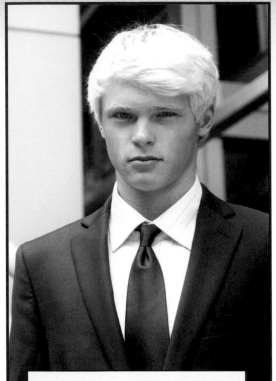

*A young man dresses neatly for his court appearance. Wearing clothing that is neat, clean, and respectful shows that you understand the seriousness of the charges against you.*

time for unexpected traffic or parking delays. If you are late for your appearance, the judge might tell you to come back another day.

When you arrive, expect to wait in line. The court will have scheduled other cases for the same day. You will have to wait until the cases scheduled ahead of you have been heard by the court. Sometimes your wait can be several hours. It is advisable to arrive early.

## STATEMENT OF RIGHTS

When you arrive, the court's clerk may give you a form called a statement of rights. You will have to read and sign this statement. It includes information about your rights to an attorney, not to incriminate yourself, to a trial, to call witnesses, and to appeal after a trial. Signing the statement shows that you understand your rights. It does not mean that you are admitting guilt.

In some courts, the statement of rights is read to all of the defendants in attendance at the same time. It may also be presented by video or audiotape. The judge in your case will ask you if you have read or heard your rights and if you understand them.

# CONSOLIDATED CASES

If there were other people cited with you, the court can hear all of the cases together as consolidated or companion cases. It is more efficient to hear the facts of the same event at the same time. For example, if you and several friends are charged with vandalism for painting graffiti on the school, the court can combine the cases. It will hear them at the same time. If your case is consolidated, everyone cited will appear in court together.

# COURTROOM FACES

Inside the courtroom, you will encounter several people. The judicial officer presides over your case. Depending on your location, this officer may be a judge, a commissioner, a magistrate, or a hearing officer. In some places, you can find out who will be hearing your case in advance. If you can, you might be able to research a judge on the court's website or in the local newspaper.

In the courtroom, the clerk works closely with the judge. The clerk prepares, finds, and files the paperwork for your case. In some cases, the clerk also collects fines. The bailiff is responsible for courtroom security. He or she wears a law enforcement uniform and is armed. In some cases, there will be someone for the prosecution. The prosecution can be a district attorney, a city attorney, or a probation officer. The prosecution presents the case against you.

Other people that may be in the courtroom include counselors, school liaisons, probation officers, and interpreters. Some courts have counselors to speak with defendants before or after the hearing. The judge may talk with a counselor before ruling on a case. In some cases, the court may have a school liaison present. The liaison is the contact between the court and your school. He or she will get your school records and talk to school counselors. A juvenile court usually has probation officers. A probation officer investigates a minor's background and presents the results to the judge. A probation officer may recommend sentences to the judge. Probation officers also follow up with you after sentencing to make sure you are following your probation orders. If you or your parents use sign language or do not speak English, you can request an interpreter for the hearing so that you can fully understand the court proceedings.

In a juvenile case, there is no jury. A judge will make decisions about your case. If you are being tried in adult court, your case might be heard by a jury.

# IN THE COURTROOM

Once in the courtroom, everything you do reflects on your character and credibility. You should be polite and respectful to everyone around you. Remain seated quietly and wait for your turn to talk. When someone else is speaking, try your best not to interrupt no matter how nervous or upset you are. When you have counsel, your lawyer will generally speak on your behalf. You should only address the court directly when your lawyer or the judge instructs you to do so.

A judge talks to a defendant, while a bailiff stands nearby.
The bailiff makes sure that the courtroom is safe and secure
during a hearing.

While you are in the courtroom, think about the attitude that you are projecting to other people present. Are you rolling your eyes or talking back to court personnel? Are you mad about being there? Without saying a word, your attitude can make the wrong impression with the court. It can show the judge that you do not understand the importance of the situation.

When it is your turn to speak, try to be calm and respectful. When you address the judge, you should use words of respect such as "Your honor," "Ma'am," or "Sir." Your words and attitude will show the judge that you are taking the court proceedings seriously and are sorry for what you have done. Showing genuine remorse and sincerity can make a difference in your case. The judge may decide to suspend your driver's license for sixty days instead of ninety days in a traffic violation case. In a misdemeanor case, the judge may sentence you to twenty hours of community service instead of forty hours. If you are uncomfortable saying you are sorry in person, ask your lawyer if it is advisable to write a letter to the judge and present it in court.

If you are a minor, your parents or guardian will be in the courtroom with you. The court may allow them to tell the court about you, any history of problems, learning disabilities, recent traumas, or any other factors they may relate to your case. The judge will ask you questions, which should be answered honestly. If they wish, your parents can also write a letter to the judge and present it in court.

# ARRAIGNMENT

At your arraignment, the judge will tell you of the charges against you. The arraignment is not a trial. No arguments for the case are heard. Instead, the judge will determine if you understand why your behavior was wrong and why you are being charged. The judge may ask you questions such as "Do you understand why you are here in court today?"

The judge will ask you to enter a plea to the charges. You may respond in one of three ways: guilty, no contest, or not guilty. A guilty plea admits that you committed the offense charged. You waive your right to a trial by judge or jury. A conviction may appear on your driving record or criminal history. Oftentimes a guilty plea is not entered at arraignment, but rather at a future court appearance. This often occurs when negotiations between your lawyer and the prosecutor lead to a less severe charge or penalties.

You should always explore the possibility of a plea agreement before going to trial because it can often limit your exposure and your punishment. Your attorney can advise you as to whether a guilty plea would provide an appropriate or advisable resolution of your case. Again, when making such a determination, you must remind your attorney to take into consideration your future employment and education goals, your immigration status, whether you are on financial aid or receiving any government benefits, and any other factors you think are important for him or her to consider.

A plea of no contest means that you are not going to fight the charges against you. You are waiving your right to a trial by judge or jury. The conviction may appear on your driving record or criminal history. A no-contest plea cannot, however, be used as an admission of guilt in another case. For example, if you plead no contest to running a red light that also involved an auto accident, it cannot be used against you in a civil case for the accident.

A not-guilty plea means that you deny the charges and wish to fight them. The prosecution must prove the charges against you beyond a reasonable doubt. If you plead not guilty, the court will set a trial date.

*A judge listens to the evidence presented at a trial. In juvenile court, the judge will decide if the defendant is guilty or not guilty. In any court, the judge will determine sentencing.*

# THE TRIAL

The trial is your opportunity to present your side of the story. What happened and why? Who was there and what did they see?

At trial, the prosecution will generally speak first. They will present the evidence. They will also call witnesses to testify against you. After each witness testifies, your lawyer will have the chance to ask them questions. Before testifying in court, any witness—including you, if

# TRIAL CONTINUANCE

Sometimes a trial is postponed. You or the officer who cited you could ask for a postponement, called a continuance. The court will decide whether to grant the continuance. In cases of hospitalization, sickness, family emergency, and other similar situations, the court will typically grant a trial continuance.

you choose to testify—will be asked to raise his or her right hand and swear to tell the truth. The police officer who cited you and any witnesses will also be asked to swear to tell the truth. Being honest is very important. Anyone who lies under oath commits perjury, which is another punishable offense.

After the prosecution has finished, you will have your opportunity present your case. You can use documents, diagrams, and maps. Simple diagrams of an intersection can be useful in a traffic violation case. Photographs can show the scene at the time of the citation. Some courts will allow video evidence to be presented as well.

You may also bring witnesses to testify at the hearing. The witnesses must have personal knowledge of the case. Consider your witnesses carefully. A bad witness may hurt your case more than help it. Witnesses are required to tell the truth. Although you can discuss the case with witnesses, you should not tell them what to say. You may also testify yourself. The decision to testify is one of a handful of decisions that is the client's decision to make, not the lawyer's. There are a number of factors to consider when making this decision. (A jury is always instructed that a defendant is under no obligation to testify and that his or her silence cannot be held against him or her.) You should always consult with your lawyer before deciding whether to testify.

Another important reminder is that it is the prosecution's burden to prove you guilty, and you are under no obligation to present a defense. In many cases, such as if your lawyer concludes that you are winning after the prosecution presents its case, your lawyer may choose to rest without presenting a defense.

## FAILURE TO APPEAR

If you don't show up for your trial, you could wind up in even more trouble. The court might have the trial without you. This is referred to as a trial in absentia. They will listen to witness testimony and rule without you being in court. If the officer who cited you does not appear in court for the trial, your case might be dismissed. Sometimes the court will decide to grant a continuance.

## THE VERDICT

The judge or jury will listen to the evidence presented at the trial. After gathering all the facts, they make a decision about the case. A jury's decision is called a verdict. A judge's decision is called a judgment. If you are found not guilty, the charges against you will be dropped. If you are found guilty, the court will decide your punishment at a subsequent court appearance.

# CHAPTER 5

# AVOIDING TROUBLE IN THE FUTURE

The sentencing phase of a hearing is called the disposition phase. If you are found guilty at your trial, the judge will decide on your fine and other consequences. To do this, the judge may ask you questions. These questions may be about your home life, school, and any problems you may have gotten into in the past. The judge may ask why you committed the offense.

## SENTENCING AND PUNISHMENT

In some cases, punishment for a misdemeanor or minor offense is mandated by law. This is called mandatory sentencing. In many cases, the court considers several factors when deciding on a punishment. Factors that affect punishment include school history, mental health, social history, and prior offenses. For example, the judge will have a copy of your record at trial. Your record shows any other offenses that you have been charged with and their dispositions. When deciding on a punishment, the judge can consider whether this is your first offense or not. He or she may decide on a more severe punishment for a teen who has been caught shoplifting for the second or third time.

*A teen attempts to shoplift a pair of sunglasses. If she has been caught shoplifting several times in the past, a judge may decide on a more severe punishment for her.*

If you are found guilty of a misdemeanor or a minor offense, there are several punishments that the court can order. Punishments include license suspensions or restrictions, fines, community service, restitution, and probation. The court may also order you to complete classes, attend therapy sessions, or write an essay. In serious cases, you may be sentenced to serve time in jail. Sometimes one or more of the these punishments, if performed prior to sentencing, will constitute a condition that once fulfilled entitles you to a lower sentence, or allows you to plead guilty to a lesser crime or receive a dismissal so long as you do not commit any future crimes in a certain period of time. The availability of these options is something you must discuss with your attorney, oftentimes before you proceed to trial or reach the sentencing phase of your case.

# LICENSE SUSPENSION OR RESTRICTION

If you are found guilty of a traffic infraction, the court may suspend, restrict, or revoke your driver's license. A license suspension means that you cannot drive under any circumstances. Sometimes the court will take your physical license. You will be able to pick it up at court after the suspension period. A license restriction allows you to drive, but only under certain conditions. For example, you may be allowed to drive to and from school or work. Sometimes the court will revoke your driver's license. If this happens, you will have to apply for a new license and go through retesting when you are allowed.

## TRAFFIC SCHOOL

Some judges will order you to attend a day of traffic school. Traffic school reviews driving laws. It also removes the offense from your permanent driving record and your insurance record. Because a driving offense on your record can increase auto insurance premiums, it is helpful to complete traffic school.

## FINES

The court may order you to pay a fine. Sometimes the fine is determined by law or local rules. Other times, the judge has some discretion over the fine amount. If you can't pay your fine on time, you can request an extension

*A teen attends traffic school as part of his punishment for a traffic violation. If he successfully completes the court-ordered traffic school, the driving offense may be removed from his permanent record.*

to pay at a later date. However, a late fee may be added to your fine.

# COMMUNITY SERVICE

In many cases, the court may order you to complete a certain number of community service hours. Community service is a wide variety of volunteer jobs that benefits your local community. Community service includes jobs such as sorting food at a food bank, graffiti cleanup, yard work at a school, or working at an animal shelter. Community service is designed to give you a sense of responsibility. It can also help you develop life and job skills that may help you in the future.

# RESTITUTION

The court may order you to pay restitution to a victim. Restitution is a sum of money that pays the victim for the monetary cost of your offense. In cases that involve property damage, restitution pays the victim for the repairs needed to fix his or her property.

# CLASSES AND DRUG TESTING

The court may also order you to attend classes or perform random drug tests. If you are found guilty of underage drinking, the court may order you to attend drug and alcohol classes. These classes will talk about the consequences of drug and alcohol abuse, understanding why people use drugs and alcohol, and learning how to deal with problems without turning to drugs and alcohol. If your offense involved tobacco, you may be ordered to take a smoking awareness class. These classes present the dangers of tobacco, dependency, and provide tips for quitting.

If your offense involves illegal drugs, the court may order you to submit to periodic drug testing. It will refer you to an authorized lab for the testing. When you arrive at the lab for your test, tell the technician about any over-the-counter or prescription drugs that you are taking that may affect your test.

If you have a history of substance abuse, the court may order you to complete a long-term rehabilitation program. Sometimes the court will refer you to a specific facility. Other times, it will allow you and your parents to choose a rehabilitation facility. Long-term rehabilitation programs can last between two to twelve months. Many rehabilitation programs are inpatient, although some may treat patients as outpatients.

## THERAPY

In some cases, the court will order you to attend therapy. For many teens, acting out is a signal that something is wrong in their life. For example, a teen who throws a chair at an adult in school may be acting out because of feelings of inferiority. A youth who takes a relative's car and is caught driving without a license may be dealing with an underlying emotional issue. Talking with a neutral counselor in therapy may help you identify why you are acting out and getting in trouble. The counselor can help you identify ways to deal with your problems in a more effective and productive way.

The court may also order you to attend hospital or morgue programs. Spending time in these facilities can quickly show teens the devastating effects that bad decisions can have on one's life. Other options include stress and anger management, tolerance programs, diversion, behavior modification programs, and parenting classes.

*A group of teens attends a court-ordered therapy session. The trained counselors work with the teens to help them avoid legal trouble in the future.*

## PLACEMENTS AND JAIL

In some serious cases, the court may order for a minor to be removed from his or her home and sent to a placement facility. A placement can be a group home, psychiatric hospital, or foster care.

The court may order a minor to spend time in a juvenile hall or youth detention center. A juvenile hall is a

49

secure, short-term detention facility for young people. A judge may send a minor involved in offenses such as drug possession or robbery to juvenile hall when waiting for a court hearing or long-term placement program.

For the most serious cases, the court may order you to spend time in jail. Prison is the most severe form of detention for youths.

# RETURNING TO COURT

After you have completed the conditions of your court order, you will return to court. Showing compliance with all court orders means the end of your court case. Compliance is obeying the orders of the court. Completing the court's orders is an accomplishment. It shows the court that you successfully followed guidelines and that you have set and accomplished goals. When you return to court, make sure you have paperwork that shows that you have completed all court orders.

If you were placed on formal probation, your probation officer will present a report to the court about you. It will include your attendance and grades at school, drug test results, and any probation violations. The probation officer's report will also have a recommendation to the court about your case.

# COURT RECORDS

In general, juvenile law enforcement records are kept confidential in most states. All states have exceptions to this rule. Some common exceptions make law enforcement records available in certain situations to courts, other law enforcement agencies, agencies responsible for a juvenile, probation departments, penal institutions, parents or legal guardians, certain school officials, and attorneys involved in the case. In addition, some states allow delinquency hearings to be open to the public.

Having a misdemeanor on your record can lead to potential consequences in the future. You may be denied a driver's license or rejected by a college or the armed services. A potential employer may even choose not to hire you.

# SEALING RECORDS

In order to keep your record private, you can request to have your records sealed or expunged. Juvenile records are not automatically sealed upon completion of probation or at a certain age. You must file a petition to get your records sealed. You should contact the local juvenile court or the juvenile probation department. States and jurisdictions vary on when and if they will allow juvenile records to be sealed. The court or probation department will look at your record and determine whether it can accommodate your request. Some records are not eligible to be sealed. Once a record has been sealed, the police, probation department, and court cannot release information about it. In most states, when your record has been sealed or expunged, it is as if the violation never occurred. For example, on a job application, you can legally respond that you have never been convicted of a crime. Regardless of how much time has passed, remember that violations are not considered crimes, and therefore the answer on a job application will always be that you have never been convicted of a crime. If asked, courts, agencies, and law enforcement are required to answer that no record exists.

It is important to know, however, that even when a record is sealed, law enforcement, government agencies and similar bodies will still be able to view it. The benefit is that private institutions and employers will not be able to view your record. Not all states expunge or seal records, and it is important to verify that your record is sealed both with the state and with the FBI.

## RIGHT TO APPEAL

If a judge finds you guilty of a misdemeanor or a minor offense, you have a right to appeal the ruling. Appeal procedures vary from jurisdiction to jurisdiction. An appeal may be a new hearing in the same court or an appellate court. The right to appeal has a time limit. If you are going to appeal, you may have as little as ten days to file the appeal, depending on your state and local laws.

You should also be aware that a decision to enter a guilty plea might require you to waive your right to appeal. You should always verify with your lawyer what rights you are potentially waiving when you enter a guilty plea. Nonetheless, a waiver of the right to appeal does not mean in all cases that you cannot appeal either your sentence or your conviction. You should consult an appellate lawyer to determine whether you may still be able to pursue on appeal on any grounds, such as the ineffective assistance of your previous attorney.

# AVOIDING FUTURE TROUBLE

Many people make mistakes. It's how you choose to learn from your mistakes that sets you apart from others. If you find yourself in a situation where you've broken the law, use it as a life lesson. Examine the event and your actions. What have you learned from your mistake? How can you change your life and behavior in order to avoid trouble in the future?

According to experts in juvenile justice, there are two important factors that have a significant influence on

*Choosing your friends wisely is a critical part of staying out of trouble. A good friend will try to talk you out of making a mistake that could land you in trouble with the law.*

whether a person returns to court for future trouble: friends and family. Relying on your family can help you make the right decisions. In addition, much of how a teen thinks and acts is influenced by his or her friends. Choosing friends wisely is one of the best ways to stay out of trouble. A good friend will talk you out of a mistake, not encourage you to make one. Sometimes being a good friend means knowing when it is time to get an adult involved, particularly in situations where serious harm could occur.

# LEARN FROM THE EXPERIENCE

If you are charged with a misdemeanor or a minor offense, you can use the experience to help you make better choices in the future. Learning about the legal system will help you achieve the best possible outcome in your case. Then you can use your experiences to make positive changes in your life, putting you on the path toward a bright future.

# GLOSSARY

**appeal** A request to a higher court to review a lower court's decision.

**arraignment** A hearing in court where the defendant hears the charges against him or her and enters a plea of guilty or not guilty.

**citation** An official summons to appear before a court.

**continuance** A postponement of a hearing to a later date.

**defendant** A person charged in a legal action.

**dismiss** To drop the charges against a defendant and terminate the case, as if it never happened.

**disposition** The final resolution of a case.

**expunged** Erased, as in records.

**felony** A serious criminal offense that is punishable by a prison sentence of more than one year.

**fine** An amount of money that is required to be paid as punishment for an offense.

**hearing** A proceeding before a court.

**infraction** The least serious offense that does not have jail time as a penalty.

**jurisdiction** The right to arrest and punish criminals.

**legal guardian** An adult who has been formally given the right to make legal decisions for a minor.

**misdemeanor** A criminal offense that is punishable by a jail sentence of one year or less.

**plea** A defendant's response to a criminal charge.

**restitution** To pay a sum of money to make amends for an injury or loss.

**sealing records** The process by which minors' criminal records are closed to public view and cannot be opened without a court order.

**violation** A type of offense that is not considered a crime and will be erased from a person's record after a period of time, generally one year.

**witness** Someone who has direct knowledge relevant to an event.

Campaign for Youth Justice (CFYJ)
1220 L Street NW, Suite 605
Washington, DC 20005
(202) 558-3580
Website: http://www.campaignforyouthjustice.org
CFYJ is a nonprofit organization that offers resources to help
    teens navigate the criminal justice system.

Canadian Department of Justice
180 Elgin Street, 7th Floor
Ottawa, ON K1A 0H8
Canada
Website: http://canada.justice.gc.ca
The Canadian Department of Justice works to ensure that
    Canada's justice system is as fair, accessible, and efficient
    as possible.

Centre for Children and Families in the Justice System
254 Pall Mall Street, Suite 200
London, ON N6A 5P6
Canada
(519) 679-7250
Website: http://www.lfcc.on.ca
The Centre for Children and Families in the Justice System of
    the London Family Court Clinic is a nonprofit agency
    that advocates for the special needs of children and fam-
    ilies involved in the justice system.

Coalition for Juvenile Justice
1319 F Street NW, Suite 402
Washington, DC 20004

(202) 467-0864

Website: http://www.juvjustice.org

CJJ is a nationwide coalition of advisory groups dedicated to
protecting the rights of youth involved in the legal
system.

National Center for Juvenile Justice

3700 South Water Street, Suite 200

Pittsburgh, PA 15203

(412) 227-6950

Website: http://www.ncjj.org

NCJJ is a private, nonprofit organization that provides information for professionals in the juvenile justice system.

Office of Juvenile Justice and Delinquency Prevention (OJJDP)

810 7th Street NW

Washington, DC 20531

(202) 307–5911

Website: http://www.ojjdp.gov

OJJDP supports states, local communities, and tribal jurisdictions in their efforts to develop and implement effective
programs for juveniles.

# WEBSITES

Because of the changing nature of Internet links, Rosen
Publishing has developed an online list of websites related
to the subject of this book. This site is updated regularly.
Please use this link to access the list:

http://www.rosenlinks.com/KYR/Misd

# FOR FURTHER READING

Bergman, Paul, and Sara J. Berman. *The Criminal Law Handbook: Know Your Rights, Survive the System.* Berkeley, CA: NOLO, 2013.

Brezina, Corona. *Careers in Law Enforcement.* New York, NY: Rosen Publishing, 2010.

Brezina, Corona. *Careers in the Juvenile Justice System.* New York, NY: Rosen Publishing, 2010.

Feinman, Jay M. *Law 101.* Oxford, England: Oxford University Press, 2010.

Furi-Perry, Ursula. *Constitutional Law for Kids: Discovering the Rights and Privileges Granted by the U.S. Constitution.* Chicago, IL: American Bar Association, 2014.

Gifis, Steven H. *Dictionary of Legal Terms: A Simplified Guide to the Language of Law.* Hauppauge, NY: Barron's Educational Series, 2008.

Hamilton, Jill. *Juvenile Crime.* Detroit, MI: Greenhaven Press, 2009.

Harmon, Daniel E. *Careers in the Corrections System.* New York, NY: Rosen Publishing, 2010.

Hudson, David L. *The Handy Law Answer Book.* Detroit, MI: Visible Ink, 2010.

Lankford, Ronald D. *Alternatives to Prisons.* Detroit, MI: Greenhaven Press, 2012.

Sax, Robin. *The Complete Idiot's Guide to the Criminal Justice System.* New York, NY: Alpha, 2009.

Vaughan, Jenny. *Juvenile Crime.* Mankato, MN: Smart Apple Media, 2012.

Ventura, John. *Law for Dummies.* Hoboken, NJ: Wiley Publishing, 2005.

# BIBLIOGRAPHY

Baird, Ben. "Saline Police: Teen Faces Multiple Misdemeanors for Spray Painting Spree, May Face Jail Time." Heritage.com, July 8, 2013.  Retrieved June 26, 2014 (http://www.heritage.com).

Baker, Robert A. "Syracuse Teen Who Police Said Falsely Reported His Abduction Faces Misdemeanor Charge." *Post-Standard*, August 18, 2012. Retrieved June 26, 2014 (www.syracuse.com).

Barrett, Carla J. *Courting Kids: Inside an Experimental Youth Court.* New York, NY: New York University Press, 2013.

Bergman, Paul. *Criminal Law: A Desk Reference.* Berkeley, CA: NOLO, 2012.

Feld, Barry C. *Kids, Cops, and Confessions: Inside the Interrogation Room.* New York, NY: New York University Press, 2012.

Krygier, Leora. *Juvenile Court: A Judge's Guide for Young Adults and Their Parents,* Lanham, MD: The Scarecrow Press, 2009.

McKenzie, James D. *McKenzie's Warning: A Criminal Defense Attorney's Game Plan for Empowering Your Teens to Protect Their Rights.* Bessemer, MI: Biblio Resource Publications, 2009.

Muller, Jeff. "Gallon Smashing Prank Videos a Hit but Raise Legal Concerns." ABC News, February 28, 2013. Retrieved June 23, 2014 (http://abcnews.go.com).

Siegel, Larry J., and Brandon Welsh. *Juvenile Delinquency: Theory, Practice, and Law.* Belmont, CA: Cengage Learning, 2012.

Simkins, Sandra. *When Kids Get Arrested: What Every Adult Should Know.* New Brunswick, NJ: Rutgers University Press, 2009.

# INDEX

## A

absentia, trial in, 42
age of majority, 13
alcohol, 6, 9, 12, 20, 27, 30, 33, 47
American Bar Association, 32
anger management, 27, 48
apology letters, 28
appeals, 34, 52
appearance, waivers of, 25, 28
arraignment, 38–39
assault, 9, 12, 13
attorney, hiring an, 32

## B

bar associations, 32
behavior modification
    programs, 48
bench warrants, 20, 25

## C

central booking, 19
citations, 15–23, 29, 31, 33
city attorneys, 35
code sections, 20, 21
Cole, Dana, 5–6
community service, 8, 9, 30, 38,
    44, 46–47
consolidated cases, 35
continuances, 13, 24, 42
court appearances
        addressing judges, 37–38
        how to dress, 33
        preparing for, 24–32

    what to expect, 33–42
court orders, 50
court records, 50–51

## D

death penalties, 11
declaration, trial by, 28
Department of Motor Vehicles
    (DMV), 25
dependency courts, 13
deportation, 32
desk appearance tickets
    (DATs), 19
disposition phases, 43
district attorneys, 30, 35
driver's licenses, 6, 14, 15, 38,
    44, 45, 48, 51
driving records, 39, 45
driving under the influence
    (DUI), 9
drug testing, 28, 47–48, 50
drugs, 9, 12, 27, 28, 30, 33,
    47–48, 50

## E

emancipation, proof of, 31

## F

failure-to-appear offenses, 25
FBI, 52
felonies, defined, 9, 11
fines, 9, 11, 12, 14, 15, 17, 26, 35,
    43, 44, 45–46

fingerprinting, 19
foster care, 49
fraud schemes, 9

**G**

graffiti, 15, 35, 47
grand theft, 12
group homes, 49
guilty pleas, 38–39

**I**

immigration lawyers, 32
interpreters, 36

**J**

jail time, 9, 11, 12, 15,
    32, 44, 50
judge, addressing a, 37–38
jurisdictions, 13, 24, 51
juvenile courts, 12, 13
juvenile halls, 49–50

**K**

Khatib, Faysal, 4
Khatib, Omar, 4
Khatib, Zayd, 4

**L**

legal guardians, 28–29, 30, 31,
    32, 51
license, driving without a, 6,
    13–14, 15, 48
Lopez, Bobby, Jr., 7

**M**

mandatory sentencing, 43
*Miranda v. Arizona*, 21
Miranda rights, 21–22
misdemeanors and minor
    offenses
        citations for, 15–23
        definition of, 7–14
        going to court for, 43–54
        how to avoid, 24–42
        overview of, 4–6
mug shots, 19
municipal courts, 12
murder, 11

**N**

no-contest pleas, 38, 39
not-guilty pleas, 38, 39

**O**

offenses, categories of, 8–9, 11

**P**

parenting classes, 48
parole, 11
perjury, 41
permanent records, 14, 45
petty theft, 12
placement facilities, 49–50
placement workers, 31
pleas, 26, 38, 39
police courts, 12

police reports, 22–23
pranks, 4–6, 7
pre-hearing contracts, 30
probable cause, 20
probation, 9, 11, 35, 36,
    44, 50, 51
probation officers, 35, 36, 50
proof of emancipation, 31
property, destruction of, 6, 15
psychiatric hospitals, 49
public drunkenness, 9, 12

**R**

records, sealing of, 51–52
rehabilitation facilities, 28, 48
restitution, 9, 44, 47
restriction of license, 44, 45

**S**

school liaisons, 36
sealing records, 51–52
shoplifting, 6, 9, 14, 15, 43
smoking awareness classes, 47
social workers, 13, 31
statement of rights, 34–35
Supreme Court, 21
suspension of license, 25, 38,
    44, 45

**T**

theft, 9, 12
therapy, 8, 28, 44, 48
tolerance programs, 48
traffic collision reports, 23
traffic schools, 45
trespassing, 12, 13, 29
Twenty-sixth Amendment, 13

**U**

unclassified misdemeanors, 11–12
urinating, in public, 6
U.S. Constitution, 13

**V**

vandalism, 14, 35
verdicts, 42
violations, defined, 8–9

**W**

waivers of appearance, 25, 28
warrants, 20, 25
witness statements, 23
witnesses, 23, 28, 34, 40–41, 42

**Y**

youth detention centers, 49
YouTube, 4, 6

## ABOUT THE AUTHOR

Carla Mooney is a graduate of the University of Pennsylvania. She writes for young people and is the author of numerous educational books. She is interested in learning about the law and the legal process in the United States.

## ABOUT THE EXPERT REVIEWER

Lindsay A. Lewis, Esq., is a practicing criminal defense attorney in New York City, where she handles a wide range of matters, from those discussed in this series to high-profile federal criminal cases. She believes that each and every defendant deserves a vigorous and informed defense. Ms. Lewis is a graduate of the Benjamin N. Cardozo School of Law and Vassar College.

## PHOTO CREDITS

Cover Rich Legg/E+/Getty Images; cover background Christophe Rolland/Shutterstock; pp. 4–5 William Howard/Stone/Getty Images; p. 8 Scott Olson/Getty Images; p. 10 Suzanne Tucker/Shutterstock.com; p. 14 © AP Images; p. 16 Ann Worthy/Shutterstock.com; pp. 18, 22, 27, 40 bikeriderlondon/Shutterstock.com; p. 29 Trista Weibel l/E+/Getty Images; p. 31 © Spencer Grant/PhotoEdit; p. 34 pkchai/Shutterstock.com; p. 37 © iStockphoto.com/Alina555; p. 44 Steven Puetzer/Photographer's Choice/Getty Images; p. 46 Alexander Raths/Shutterstock.com; p. 49 wavebreakmedia/Shutterstock.com; p. 53 © iStockphoto.com/RonTech2000.

Designer: Brian Garvey; Editor: Jacob Steinberg